W9-BPO-992

SAN FRANCISCO

GALLERY BOOKS
An Imprint of W. H. Smith Publishers Inc.
112 Madison Avenue
New York City 10016

This edition first published in U.S.
in 1990 by Gallery Books,
an imprint of W.H. Smith Publishers, Inc.
112 Madison Avenue, New York, New York 10016

second printing

ISBN 0-8317-8830-5

Printed and bound in Spain

For rights information about the photographs in
this book please contact:

The Image Bank
111 Fifth Avenue, New York, N.Y. 10003

Producer: Solomon M. Skolnick
Author: Nancy Millichap Davies
Design Concept: Lesley Ehlers
Designer: Ann-Louise Lipman
Editor: Madelyn Larsen
Production: Valerie Zars
Photo Researcher: Edward Douglas
Assistant Photo Researcher: Robert Hale

Title page: *Symbol of its city, the Golden Gate Bridge stretches 8,940 feet
across the strait where San Francisco Bay meets the Pacific Ocean.* Above: *Dawn
tints San Francisco's skyline and the hills beyond as they rise above the fog.*

Preceding page: *Deep white fog forms off the headlands of San Francisco Bay and drifts inland.* Above: *Painters climb high above the Golden Gate's span to continue the endless task of maintaining the bridge's protective orange finish.* Left: *Suspended on cables from the Golden Gate's two 746-foot towers, a six-lane roadway and two footpaths carry traffic from Marin County to downtown San Francisco.* Opposite: *The bridge's dedicatory plaque bears its construction dates, 1933 to 1937. A bronze statue of Chief Engineer Joseph B. Strauss, with the structure that demonstrates his vision and skill in the distance.*

Through the fog-shrouded narrows called Golden Gate at the entrance to its bay, San Francisco looks toward the Pacific Ocean. Its original Spanish settlers chose the site for its inland harbor, and it owes to maritime trade its early development and its rise to prominence. A stopping place for wayfarers in search of their dreams in the days of the Gold Rush, the city acquired its reputation for tolerance of differences early. In the years since, wanderers from every point of the compass have found in the city by the bay an atmosphere of openness lacking in their homelands—or in their home towns. They have passed through, have come to work here for a time, or have stayed. In many cases, newcomers have brought with them the new ideas that keep the city looking forward. San Francisco's only constant features are its magnificent natural setting and the endless process of change, with a nod to the heritage of the past, that marks productive human society.

It seems incredible that this city, so responsive to the new, yet also so aware of the old, has existed for only a little more than two centuries. When the Spanish explorer Ortega sighted the bay in 1769, the future metropolis was nothing more than a headland covered with wild mint, home to some small villages of Costanoan Indians.

Preceding page: *Sunlight pours down on the 4,200-foot center span between the two towers of the Golden Gate Bridge, at its completion in May 1937 the world's longest single span.* Right: *A tall ship riding at anchor in Aquatic Park.* Below and opposite: *"The Rock" to a generation of the most hardened felons in the federal prison system, the cells of Alcatraz once confined such famous criminals as Al Capone and Robert Stroud, the Birdman of Alcatraz. Now the island is part of the Golden Gate Recreation Area.*

The city's first European residents arrived in 1776, a band of settlers, soldiers, and priests led by Juan Bautista de Anza. Soon the tiny settlement had its military headquarters and its church, the Presidio and the Mission San Francisco de Asis. The site of that original Presidio remains a military reservation today. The mission has always more commonly been called by the name of a small nearby lake filled in long ago, Laguna de los Dolores, or Lake of Sorrows: Mission Dolores. Its four-foot-thick adobe walls stand under their roof of brown tiles, little changed in appearance, in the midst of a vibrant district that is still mostly Spanish-speaking.

The first settlers called their village on the cove Yerba Buena, or "good grass," possibly in honor of the abundantly growing mint. Cultivated crops were less successful. With dry scrub-covered hills rising just behind it, Yerba Buena had little good farmland, and many settlers con-

Opposite: *Corinthian columns border the semicircular Palace of Fine Arts, sole surviving building of the Panama-Pacific International Exposition of 1915. The elaborate Hellenic style of the building suggests the romantic fancy of a grander age. This page: Fairgoers at the Exposition viewed art treasures here. Restored as the Palace of Arts and Science, it is now home to San Francisco's Exploratorium.*

tinued down the coast to more promising fields. What growth did occur in San Francisco's first 74 years was in trade: its cove became a center for foreign shipping to nearby mission villages with poorer harbors. When Mexico broke from Spain in 1821, the remote Spanish colonial outpost became a village in the outlying Mexican province of Alta California.

In 1846, during the Mexican-American War, Yerba Buena moved from Mexican to American control. Within a few months, a Spanish-speaking

Opposite: *A formal floral display hints at the botanical riches within Golden Gate Park's Victorian glasshouse, the Conservatory of Flowers, modeled on the Royal Conservatories in London's Kew Gardens. This page: Boaters on Stow Lake, largest of Golden Gate Park's artificial lakes. Translucent walls and jewel-bright glass give the Conservatory of Flowers an ethereal look.*

American officer changed its name to San Francisco in honor of the nearby Mission San Francisco de Asis. John Charles Frémont, another American military adventurer in the area, named the three-mile strait between the San Francisco Peninsula and the Marin Peninsula to its north "Golden Gate." Frémont chose the name with a vague awareness of the possibilities of Asian trade, little suspecting how closely people throughout the world would soon associate the word "gold" with San Francisco.

Gold flecks turned up in John Sutter's millrace on the American River in 1848. The word spread fast: first to his neighborhood, then to San Francisco and other California settlements, and by 1849 to the nation and beyond. Miners seeking their fortunes descended on San Francisco, the most convenient port for the gold fields. The sleepy Spanish-speaking village became a raw, crowded tent city of men (few of the newcomers in the first year or two were women). Its population rose from about

Opposite: *Flags flutter around the 308-foot-high dome of the City Hall rotunda, focal point of the Civic Center. The 1915 granite structure covers two city blocks. This page: The Church of Saints Peter and Paul in the heart of North Beach, a district with an Italian heritage. Rodin's "The Thinker" rests at the entrance of the California Palace of the Legion of Honor, built in memory of Californians who died in World War I.*

HONNEUR ET PATRIE

California Palace
of the
Legion of Honor

This page: *A statue of Padre Junípero Serra, founder of Mission Dolores, which was completed in 1782. The 1100 block of Lombard Street runs up Russian Hill on a 27-degree grade.* Opposite: *Tidy hedges rim the flowerbeds winding uphill along the eight switchbacks in the 1100 block of Lombard Street, "the crookedest street in the world."*

860 in the days just before the Gold Rush to 42,000 by the end of 1852. For thousands of miners, the new city was a supply base, a banking center, a place to go for recreation and company, and a refuge in winter from the cold and rain of the gold fields. For bankers and tradesmen, the Gold Rush was a grand opportunity. It made the difference between San Francisco and all the other developing villages and towns of California in the mid-nineteenth century, bringing prosperity and growth beyond the dreams of even the biggest boosters of the little seaport.

This gold-rush boom coincided with the advent of steamship travel, which by the end of the century made the city a major world port. Clipper ships were developed in part to speed the "Argonauts" —those sailing in quest of gold—on their way around the Horn. Once in San Francisco, many ships' crews abandoned their vessels in the harbor and headed for the gold fields themselves. As gold production petered out, the city turned from dropoff point and supply depot for the mining industry

Opposite: *A coffee shop at the corner of Haight and Ashbury Streets, an intersection whose name came to symbolize the counterculture of the 1960s.* This page: *Large outdoor murals in the Mission District reflect the traditions of Hispanic art. Brilliant colors, strong contrasts, and bold designs make for arresting folk art.*

Preceding pages: Turn-of-the-century townhouses on Steiner Street contrast with the downtown skyline. Opposite: The shopping district on fashionable Union Street. This page: Sunset on Nob Hill. Noe Valley rowhouses are always distinctive in color and ornament even if often identical in shape.

to outfitter for the whaling trade and hub of Pacific commerce. While the Embarcadero sees fewer cargo ships today than in the past, the city well remembers that trade goods and immigrants arriving by water historically have been its source of fortune. In a city where almost every hill offers a vista of ocean or bay, what resident or visitor can forget such important origins?

Shipping made San Francisco, but even as the city rose to prominence as a port, a new means of overland transportation was gaining world-wide importance. The railroad would provide the second impetus of San Francisco's growth. By 1860, with production from the gold mines declining, the local economy needed a boost. A group of four Sacramento merchants with only about $50,000 among them seized the opportunity, founding the Central Pacific Company. Soon Central Pacific was racing against other fledgling rail companies to join the country's first transcontinental span. In 1869, eastern and western rails met at Promontory Point, Utah, and San Francisco was considerably less isolated from

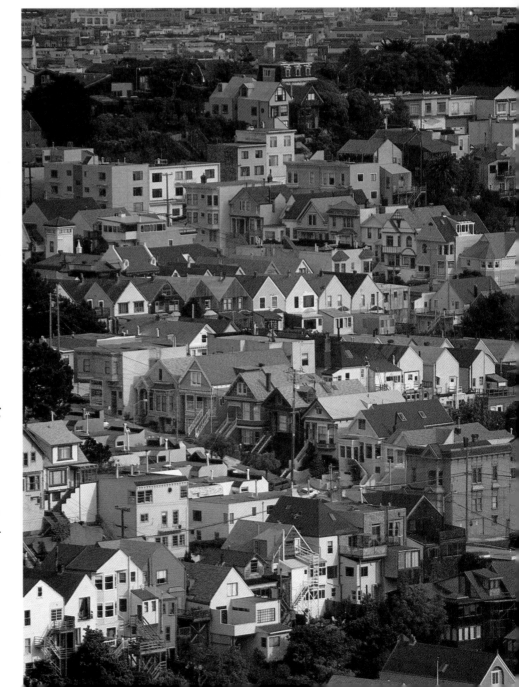

the rest of the country. The merchants—Mark Hopkins, Charles Crocker, Leland Stanford, and Collis P. Huntington—became overnight millionaires known locally as the Big Four. Their elaborate homes, heavy with the carved "gingerbread" decoration of high Victorian style, soon capped San Francisco's hilltops. Other newly rich businessmen joined in the construction rivalry. The very name Nob Hill, site of the grandest of these mansions, refers to the "nabobs" of commercial enterprise who built them. The

In the Financial District, an elaborate Edwardian bowfront (left) and the Phelan Building (right) present a sharp contrast in color and style to the starkly contemporary buildings below. Opposite: The 48-story Transamerica Pyramid built in 1972.

mansions themselves burned, one after another, in the fires after the earthquake of 1906. Only a Connecticut brownstone, now the Pacific Union Club, escaped the flames. Apartment blocks and grand hotels, including today's Fairmont and Mark Hopkins, took their places.

Nob Hill would have remained inaccessible and undeveloped if it were not for a form of transportation designed just for San Francisco by another of the city's resourceful immigrants. English-born engineer Andrew Hallidie invented the cable car in 1871 specifically to convey people and goods up hills too steep for horses. Today his invention is second only to the Golden Gate as a symbol of the city. The open cars, some in use since the 1890s, carry 34 seated passengers, plus standees, at a speed of 9½ miles per hour. A central powerhouse at Mason and Washington Streets controls the steel cables that drive the cars; these cables run in channels 18 inches below the surface of the road. Newer

The cable car was invented in 1871 to make accessible the many San Francisco hills too steep for horse-drawn vehicles. Opposite: A Powell-Hyde cable car makes the grade on its way to Fisherman's Wharf. Overleaf: Near the Fisherman's Wharf terminus, a conductor signals to the gripman (driver) in preparation for a switching maneuver.

HYDE Sts.

B A Y L E Y

THE PER
NIGHT

BAILEYS
ORIGINAL IRISH CREAM

Baileys Original Irish Cream Liqueur® Imported by The Paddington Corporation, Fort Lee, N.J. 17% alc. by vol. • 1987

N FRANCISCO MUNICIPAL

technologies such as the electric streetcar and the automobile have long since surpassed the cable car in speed and efficiency, but popular enthusiasm for the cars has kept three of the original twelve lines in operation. Daily, upwards of 40,000 passengers ride the ten miles of the system, which was named a National Historic Landmark in 1964 and completely renovated in 1984.

Little more than a half century ago, journeys between San Francisco and other communities around the bay were possible only by ferryboat. As many as 50,000,000 people annually passed through the Ferry Terminal under its clock tower at the Embarcadero. Then, in the 1930s, two great steel bridges spanned the bay. The first of these to be completed (in 1936) was the San Francisco–Oakland Bay Bridge, which allowed direct ground transportation to the east bay for the first time and gave direct access to the transcontinental

Above: *The Fairmont, Nob Hill's first grand hotel, was under construction in 1906; only its white granite walls survived post-earthquake fires. Restored, it opened one year later.* Below: *The 20-story Mark Hopkins Hotel, built in 1926, carries the name of the railroad baron whose mansion once occupied the site.* Opposite: *The glass dome that topped the rotunda of the City of Paris department store (1908) has a new home at Nieman-Marcus (1983), which occupies the same site.*

rail lines that end in Oakland. The Golden Gate Bridge, designed by Ohioan Joseph Strauss and completed in 1937, swept north, connecting downtown San Francisco to Marin County. Its picturesque setting, splendid design, record-setting span, and apparent fragility have combined to make it a world-famous emblem of the city beside the bay.

The addition of bridges to the skyline represents only one of the city's continual transformations. One vital section of downtown has worn a new aspect in each era of San Francisco's development: the Financial District behind the Embarcadero. In Gold Rush days, the first office buildings in the city rose here. While some fine examples of buildings from the 1850s and 1860s remain in the Jackson Historic District, a four-square-block area north of today's Financial District, most Victorian-era buildings in the area burned in the fires after the 1906 earthquake. In the feverish rush to rebuild,

Above: *The War Memorial Opera House at the Civic Center, home of the San Francisco Opera Company. Completed in 1932, it was the first municipally owned Opera House in the United States.*
Center: *The San Francisco Museum of Modern Art has in its distinguished collection the works of such masters as Rivera and Picasso.*
Below: *The California Academy of Sciences, Golden Gate Park. The complex includes a natural history museum, aquarium (opposite), and planetarium.*

CON D O

BIG
AL'S

NUDE
GIRLS

RITA
RICARD
X
STAR

LOVE ACT

BIG AL'S

TOTALLY NUDE
GIRLS ON STAGE

TOTALLY NUDE

SEXSATIONAL

ARING

20's

the steel frames of some newer buildings that had survived were given new exteriors, and dozens of new commercial buildings rose alongside them. Many of these post-earthquake steel-frame buildings, well-proportioned, light-colored "skyscrapers" of ten to twenty stories, survive downtown today, dwarfed by surrounding high-rises.

In the late 1960s, the Financial District's architectural landscape was once again drastically revised. Banks and other financial institutions managing the mushrooming trade with the nations of the Pacific Rim sought expanded quarters. Large-scale urban redevelopment set in. Its most obvious results include the newest of the city's distinctive symbols, the unmistakable lines of the Transamerica Pyramid, and the four slender towers of Embarcadero Center, which tower above the 1898 Ferry Building. Further west along the waterfront, change has been more evolutionary. Nineteenth-century brick factories behind Fisherman's Wharf have been remodeled as complexes of shops and restaurants.

North Beach's Broadway, birthplace of topless nightclubs (opposite). This page: Chinatown seems half a world away from the Transamerica Pyramid in the Financial District. Jackson Street is in the heart of Chinatown, reputedly the largest Chinese settlement outside the Orient.

Not all changes to the cityscape have been deliberate. Throughout the nineteenth century, the city, positioned just beyond the end of the San Andreas Fault, experienced numerous earthquakes and fires. With redwood the most abundant building material, at the turn of the twentieth century over 90 percent of San Francisco's buildings were made of wood, and fires were particularly disastrous. The most famous calamity ever to befall San Francisco, in fact, had two components: the earthquake of April 1906 and the resulting fire. The quake,

A dragon, Chinatown's official protector since the earliest days of immigration, keeps a watchful eye on this newsstand. Below: Marchers animate a 150-foot-long paper dragon during a festive parade on the seventh day of the Chinese New Year. Opposite: Wearing traditional dress, young Japanese-American women play the shamisen, *a stringed instrument not unlike the banjo. Below: Mixed messages. Above the English notice banning advertisements on this Chinatown wall, an ad in Chinese characters promises quick service at a photo-developing shop*

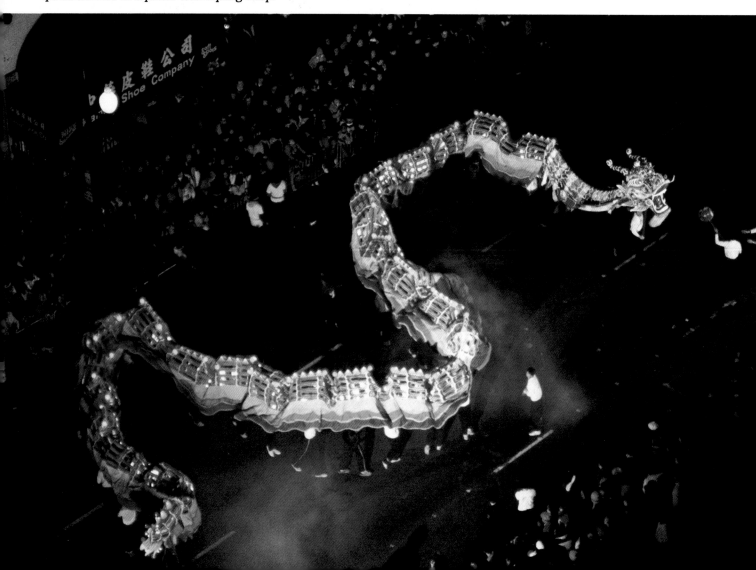

which probably would have measured 8.3 on the Richter scale (which had not yet been invented), began around 5 a.m. with most citizens still in bed. Buildings destroyed by the quake itself included the recently completed City Hall, where the dome hung oddly from the few supporting columns still upright, but the fires that followed brought widespread destruction. Many of the toppling wooden buildings contained lighted lamps and woodstoves, starting fires in dozens of places. Fire companies rushed to the blazes only to find that the hydrants, connected to broken water mains, were useless. The conflagration raged for three days. To stop it, the firefighters resorted to a desperate act: blowing up the entire line of mansions along Van Ness Avenue. When the flames died at last, they had destroyed 28,000 buildings over an area of 500 square blocks, more than three-fifths of the city, and had left at least a quarter of a million people homeless. In one way, though, the disaster brightened San Francisco's future. The city, rebuilt almost instantaneously, was much sounder and more modern than the one it replaced, better designed for a role as the premier U.S. Pacific port. It would retain that status through World War II.

The city's reputation for tolerance, as well as its scenic attractiveness, made it the

A two-story gate arches over the eastern entrance to Golden Gate Park's Japanese Tea Garden, five acres of Japanese and Chinese plantings and landscape design. The bronze Buddha cast in Japan in 1790 was given by art dealers Gump & Co. in 1949. Opposite: In Union Square, an oasis of palms and plantings in the heart of the shopping district, Victory crowns the Dewey Monument. It stood firm through the 1906 earthquake.

home of a major movement of popular culture that began during the Cold War years and played itself out by the mid-1970s. Intellectual newcomers from the East Coast, the Beats or hipsters, converged on North Beach in the 1950s. They gathered in bookshops and coffeehouses to read outrageus poetry, listen to jazz, and seek their identities. The Beats were succeeded by hippies, young men and women from across the nation who migrated to Haight-Ashbury for the 1967 "Summer of Love." They believed that free sexual expression, rock music, and the use of hallucinogens would result in a revolution and bring in a new society of peace and love. The movement's naïve idealism was soon corrupted by greedy drug pushers, overdoses, overcrowding, violence, and disease. By the beginning of the 1970s, widely publicized casualties of the movement led to the popular realization that drug use was, in fact, not a path to enlightenment. Most of the hippies went back home or

Opposite: *Festive lights adorn the clock tower of the Ferry Building, the waterfront landmark that has greeted passengers arriving at the Embarcadero since 1898.*
Above: *Among the world's busiest harbors in the steamship era, the Port of San Francisco is surrounded today by the gleaming towers of downtown redevelopment.*
Below: *Just behind the Fisherman's Wharf waterfront, Ghirardelli Square houses elegant shops and restaurants in the renovated chocolate factory.*

Focal point in this panoramic shot, the 210-foot Coit Memorial Tower (center) rises from the top of Telegraph Hill. Constructed in 1933, it is a memorial to the city's volunteer firefighters and has WPA murals within. Opposite: A statue of Christopher Columbus, whose national origin endears him to Telegraph Hill's Italian-Americans, looks seaward amid Pioneer Park's flowerbeds.

back to school, the Vietnam War ended, and eventually Haight-Ashbury became once more the middle-class area that it had been in the 1940s. As in many of San Francisco's restored Victorian neighborhoods, a sizeable minority of the Haight's population is gay (citywide the gay population is perhaps 15 percent). The city's reputation for openness, along with the passage of a landmark gay-rights city ordinance in 1977, have made it a center of homosexual and lesbian culture.

Most U.S. cities had large immigrant quarters in the nineteenth century, but only San Francisco had a Chinatown. In 1848 there were no Chinese in California; ten years later there were 25,000. These first Chinese immigrants, fleeing floods and famine in their country, provided labor in the gold fields. When gold production slowed, they found work laying the transcontinental railroad. After its completion, some San Franciscans who came to view the Chinese willingness to work for low wages as a threat to their own

jobs pressured their representatives to restrict immigration. The resulting Chinese Exclusion Act shut it off altogether in 1882. Those Chinese already in the country remained, often continuing to live much as they had in China. An organization known as the Six Companies regulated political and social life in Chinatown throughout much of the nineteenth century. In more recent years assimiliation has proceeded for the Chinese as for other ethnic groups, but the area remains the city's most distinctive ethnic section, with San Franciscans and visitors alike flocking to its restaurants and shops and lining the streets for its New Year's Parade. Close ties with Asia continue: 11 percent of Chinatown residents as recently as 1980 were born in China.

The Chinese were by no means the sole ethnic group to play an important and still visible role in the city's development. The Japanese, too, emigrated to the Pacific coast of the United States in the nineteenth century. Unlike the Chinese, they

A Fisherman's Wharf chef smiles above a steaming plate of Dungeness crabs (opposite). This page: *At Fisherman's Wharf, working boats moor near restaurants that serve millions of visitors annually. Ferries take sightseers out to view the waterfront, bridges, and islands in San Francisco.*

Preceding page: *Against a background of dark sky, this panorama of post 1960s high-rises presents the Financial District's new face.* This page: *The office towers of Embarcadero Center soar above the waterfront.* Below: *Yerba Buena and the Treasure Islands glitter in the bay beyond. The lights of Berkeley rim the far shore.* Opposite: *One Embarcadero Center in profile, framed by one of the many modern sculptures in the plazas.*

developed no permanent association with a particular area of the city, in part because of their internment as alleged supporters of the enemy during World War II. In the internment camps, many Japanese lost their property and their prosperity. Today's Japantown was created in the 1960s as part of an urban renewal project. While its sleek contemporary buildings provide headquarters for Japanese cultural and artistic institutions, Japanese-Americans live elsewhere, widely dispersed throughout the city and its suburbs.

Another principal immigrant group was the Italians, who dominated the fishing trade for decades, setting forth to open sea through the Golden Gate in boats of Mediterranean design. Italian culture flourished in North Beach around the church of Saints Peter and Paul. Today, many of Fisherman's Wharf's

Opposite: *An Embarcadero Center office tower fills the sky. In the foreground, one of the square concrete pipes of Vaillancourt Fountain.* This page: *Philip Johnson's 23-story office building at 580 California Street is a 1983 addition to the Financial District and was designed to blend with its older neighbors. Hooded statues swing their stony draperies high above the city at the roofline. The nearby Bank of America tower rises in the background.*

The Transamerica Pyramid. The tallest office building (853 feet) in the city, it dominates the skyline. A hollow 212-foot spire caps its 48 stories. The Transamerica Pyramid, viewed from below. Three thousand concrete panels, each weighing 3½ tons, make up the curtain walls, which slope inward at a 5-degree angle.

The San Francisco–Oakland Bay Bridge. Built by the State of California with New Deal funds in 1936, the bridge's 8¼-mile length includes two suspension bridges, a tunnel, and a cantilevered span. Overleaf: A view of the waterfront above Bay Bridge cables.

finest restaurants bear Italian names. Italians also founded local industries: in chic Ghirardelli Square hangs the huge electric sign that in 1926 was first lighted above the Ghirardelli Chocolate Factory, legible then (and now) to shipping in the bay.

Wanderers—today we call them travelers, or perhaps tourists—still come, from other parts of the United States and from other countries as well. They have heard that they will find in San Francisco a unique combination of lovely vistas, old-fashioned architectural charm, elegant urban ambience, and the multicultural richness of a great international city. The travelers are expected: San Franciscans know that new-comers will be arriving tomorrow, and that their influence will keep the city by the Golden Gate at the fore-front of growth and change.

Opposite: *The Richmond–San Rafael Bay Bridge, opened in 1956, spans San Pablo Bay. An 1875 lighthouse on Yerba Buena Island in midbay offers westward vistas of the Bay Bridge and of downtown San Francisco.* This page: *Looking west over Oakland. The city where the transcontinental rails ended remains a leading industrial and transport center.* Below: *In the center of Sausalito, the Marin County community just beyond the northern end of the Golden Gate bridge, an elephant statue adds charm to Plaza Viña del Mar.* Overleaf: *Restaurants and shops stand on wharves that once were home port for Sausalito's fishing fleet.*

INDEX OF PHOTOGRAPHY

All photographs courtesy of The Image Bank,
except where indicated*